Summer

Bright red acer glows:

Warmth of sunny summer days

Persists to winter.

Sometimes Only Rain Will Do

Lorraine Gradwell

TBR Imprint

TBR Imprint,
26 Chapel Road,
Manchester M33 7EG, UK

www.lorrainegradwell.wordpress.com

Printed and bound by CATS Printing,
University of Salford, M5 4WT, UK

ISBN 9780957260658

This book has become a reality because of the love and support - and no small amount of encouragement - of Tony Baldwinson.

Sometimes Only Rain Will Do

Lorraine Gradwell

Introduction

A haiku is a traditional Japanese verse of just seventeen syllables, arranged in three phrases of five, seven, and five syllables respectively. Typically a haiku relates to the elements, the weather, and the natural environment.

I like the haiku as a form of poetry because I like the minimalism, the application required to condense what you want to say into the required number of syllables, and to still produce something pleasing.

My collection includes some haiku which conform to the traditional, but also a range of wider topics. I hope you like them.

Elements

Sea

Distant hazy shores
Shimmer through sea mist
blankets.
Pebbles turn in surf.

Tides #1

Relentless tides push,

Wash clattering stones away.

Crabs dodge, sheltering.

Tides #2

Rhythms deepen, waves pulse,
Rock pools fill to overflow.
The tide is turning.

Auracaria

Auracaria:

Monkey-puzzle tree. What a
Quirky name you have.

Crows

Distant hills beckon,

Rising against stormy skies.

Crows flock among oaks.

November

Canal geese congregate,
Stand in line, damply huddle.
Drizzle dripping down.

Rain #1

Constant, persistent,
Sometimes only rain will do.
Sad, yes, but soothing.

Rain #2

Overnight rain storms
Interrupt slumbering peace,
Drumming through my
dreams.

Halloween

A dull moon droops low,
Wraith-like, lonesome mist
uncurls.
Bats criss-cross the sky.

Cold sun

Autumnal morning,
Ochre-bright shafts of cold
sun.
Golden leaves tumble.

Silhouettes

Frost shadows play games,

Outline melted silhouettes.

Trees lay in the snow.

Winter

Piercing cold creeps past
Snow laden shivering boughs.
Freezing mist hangs low.

Emotions

Weather

Is it the weather?
Sharp words, exchanged in
anger,
Chill me to the core.

A rare flash

Connecting for once,
Our eyes embrace. A rare flash
Of love springs anew.

Barbed

Sweetly spoken, yet
Barbed: your words blow
through me, tear
At my self belief.

Listen

You said you'd listen,
But half my words go unheard.
'What was that?' you say.

Promises

Careless commitment,
Bitter words bring icy winds:
Broken promises.

Fragility

Your words chill my heart,
Plunder my fragility:
"It's not you, it's me".

Silence

You repay my words
With silence. Does time endure
Or will it run out?

Touch

I miss you. I need
To feel your longing for me:
I ache for your touch.

Opportunity

Opportunity

Can be hard to recognise.

Grasp it while you can.

Promises #2

Disillusionment
Saddens me, lays bare
promises
Unkept, unheeded.

Assisted suicide
haikus

Assisted suicide #1

My life examined,
Your alien gaze unkind,
I'm deemed worthless.

Assisted suicide #2

Fool if you believe

Institutionalised death

To be a kindness.

Assisted suicide #3

I can't bear your pain –
Such hurt, so undignified,
Let's end it for you.

Urban Haikus

Urban haiku #1

Noisy coffee shop:
Bacon and brie panini,
Earl grey tea, no milk.

Urban haiku #2

Clinking cups, hissing
Machines, steam clouds rising.
Skinny latte please.

Urban haiku #3

Mirrored walls glow red,
Sunset bounced by towered glass.
City evening falls.

Urban haiku #4

Singing wires herald

An imminent arrival.

Crowds will engulf you.

Urban haiku #5

Urban street colours:
Red bricks, grey pavement, blue bus,
Odd slivers of grass.

Weaving

Mist swirls among trees;
Moonrise casts ghostly
shadows.
Spiders weave, and hide.